D0108284

37653012017334
Main  NonFiction
818.5407 BEARD
French cats don't get fat :
the secrets of la cuisine
feline

FEB   2006

CENTRAL ARKANSAS LIBRARY SYSTEM
LITTLE ROCK PUBLIC LIBRARY
100 ROCK STREET
LITTLE ROCK, ARKANSAS

Bond Book

This book is one of 155,000 in a special purchase to upgrade the CALS collection. Funds for the project were approved by Little Rock voters on 8/17/04.

French Cats
Don't
Get Fat

French Cats Don't Get Fat

The Secrets of La Cuisine Féline

by Henri de la Barbe
(Henry Beard)

ILLUSTRATIONS BY SUSANN FERRIS JONES

A JOHN BOSWELL ASSOCIATES BOOK

Crown Publishers, New York

Copyright © 2005 by Henry Beard and John Boswell Management, Inc.
All rights reserved.
Published in the United States by Crown Publishers, an imprint of the
Crown Publishing Group, a division of Random House, Inc., New York.
www.crownpublishing.com

Crown is a trademark and the Crown colophon is a registered trademark of
Random House, Inc.

Library of Congress Cataloging-in-Publication Data is available
on request.

ISBN 0-307-33780-4

PRINTED IN THE UNITED STATES OF AMERICA

Book design: *Nan Jernigan*
Assitance in French Translation: Luc Brébion

10 9 8 7 6 5 4 3 2 1

FIRST EDITION

Dédicace

À la mémoire de

Cosimo, Kitty, Marie, Marvin, Moo, Motley,
Polly, Serafina, Sister Quarantina,
Tigger, *et* Tudi

CENTRAL ARKANSAS LIBRARY SYSTEM
LITTLE ROCK PUBLIC LIBRARY
100 ROCK STREET
LITTLE ROCK, ARKANSAS 72201

ALSO BY HENRY BEARD

I am a French cat.

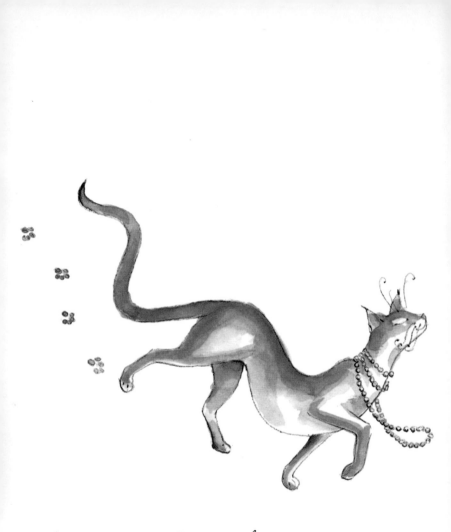

As you can see, I am not fat.

I am trim, slim, slender—what is *le mot juste*? I am *svelte*.

Why is this so?

Pourquoi am I not a huge, furry cow *comme les chats américains* and *les chats anglais?*

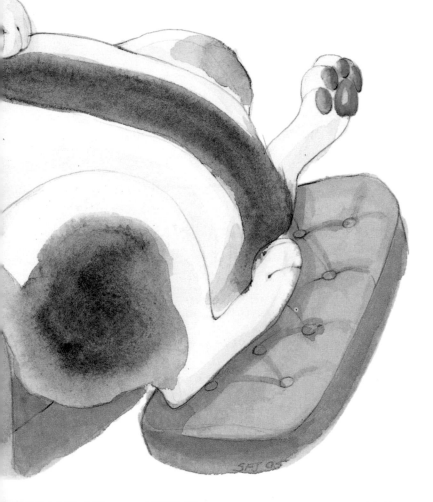

Peut-être the secret lies hidden in the mysteries of the French food *pyramide* . . .

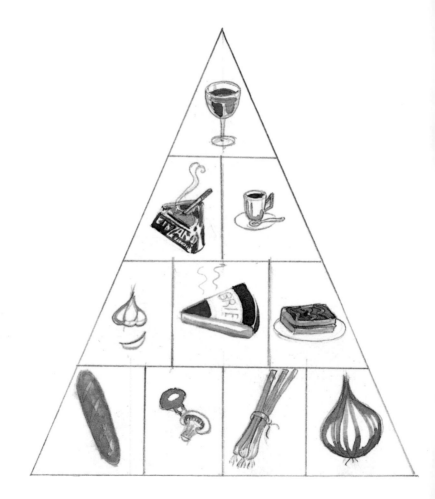

Mais non, mes amis! It is not what we eat, but how we eat, comporting ourselves as discriminating *connaisseurs,* not gluttonous *cochons.*

In short, *je propose* that you adopt a whole new way of thinking about food. Of course, if you have overindulged, as I myself once did, it is necessary first to purge oneself of all impurities.

Voilà! Now we can begin.

There is more to the art of dining well than the mere consumption of the meal. Of equal importance is the setting in which the repast is served—the *décor*, the *milieu*, the *ambiance*.

Bistro au
Bon Chat

94

Ooh, la-la! Mon plat favori! Rack of lemming, *garni! Mes compliments au chef!*

As I always practice strict portion control,
I will take the remainder home in this
handy, albeit inaptly named, "doggie" bag.

The Sensory Experience

True masterpieces of the gastronomic arts rely less on elaborate modes of preparation than on procuring the ingredients of the dish at the precise moment of ripe perfection.

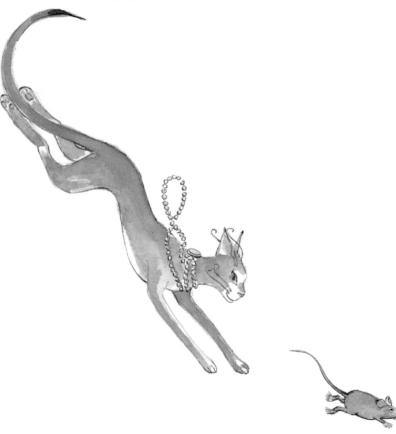

Thus, it is *très important* that your mouse—
or baby bird, or bunny, or plump little
chipmunk—be completely fresh, even a
bit on the frisky side.

Select, if possible, a small, young, unblem-
ished specimen, with bright eyes, a firm tail,
and good coloring.

Partake of your prey with *tous les sens* — sight, sound, smell, taste, and touch. Observe the *qualité de la présentation* . . .

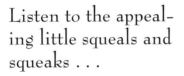

Listen to the appealing little squeals and squeaks . . .

Sniff the musty, earthy *odeurs* and the *parfum* of fear . . .

Sample the exquisite *mélange* of subtle flavors.

Relish the crunchy, grainy texture, and the delicate "mouth feel" . . .

Notez bien that I do not devour *cette petite chose* — I savor it, taking tiny little bites, chewing slowly, reveling in each and every delectable morsel.

Magnifique! Formidable!

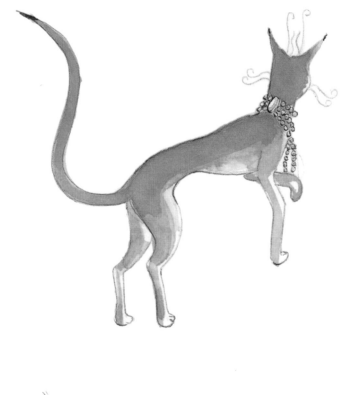

Food for Thought

Processed foods are a mundane but *inévitable* part of the diet. They are *parfaitement acceptable*, if consumed in *modération*. Eat no more than half of the dry food and scatter the rest of the nuggets *partout* on the kitchen floor.

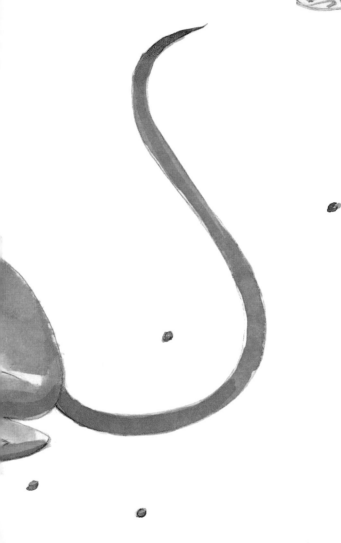

As far as wet food goes, I am happy to say that *nouvelle cuisine* appears to be a thing of the past. *Zut!*

Although we do still have spa food to contend with.

Leftovers put in your bowl by well-meaning *humains* are a dangerous temptation. Do not hesitate to spurn such "treats," but if you do consume something unsuitable, expel it from your system *tout de suite*.

A Few Simple Recipes

Ratatouille
SERVES ONE

INGREDIENTS

1 rat

1. Kill a large rat.
2. Shred thoroughly.
3. Scatter pieces on carpet.

Vole au Vent
SERVES ONE

INGREDIENTS

1 vole

1. Trap one whole vole.
2. Toss it around lightly.
3. Mince finely.

Mouse au Chocolat
SERVES ONE

INGREDIENTS

1 mouse

1. Catch one medium-size mouse.
2. Play with it for about 45 minutes.
3. Forget the chocolate.

Le Workout

Physical *activité* is a key part of a weight-management program.

Je recommande a few simple exercises. *Bon,* scamper upstairs and look around, then saunter downstairs and look around. Do this every twenty minutes.

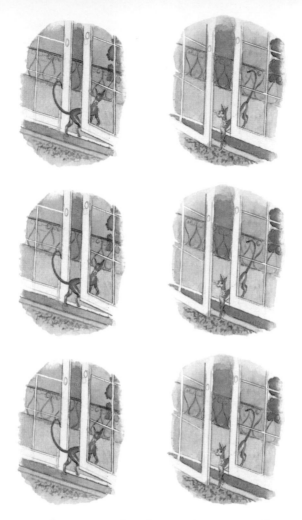

Go outside, come back in. Go outside
again, come right back in. *Dehors, dedans.
Dehors, dedans. Répétez* two hundred times.

If you have a scratch-ing post, *très bien*. Use it regularly to maintain paw tone.

If you have not been provided with *un poteau*, pick something pliable and tear it to pieces.

Run around like crazy for about sixty
seconds. To obtain the maximum benefit,
this *mouvement* should be done in no
particular direction and for no apparent
reason.

There is also nothing
like a brisk game of
boules to get the
blood flowing.

Jump up onto the couch. When instructed
to get off the couch, take your time coming down. *Alors,* wait until the count of
four and then jump *immédiatement* back on
the couch. Continue until bored.

At least once a week, make the ascent to the roof. This climb stimulates the breathing marvelously, as does the extended period of loud screaming needed to attract the attention of whoever is going to carry you down.

Le Chic

The essence of style is, less is more. And since, *sans doute*, you possess, as I do, the ultimate *accoutrement*—a *superbe* fur coat—I admonish you to exercise restraint in wardrobe accessories. Confine yourself to a simple strand of pearls . . .

Dior

Chanel

An understated flea-and-tick collar from a recognized *couturier* . . .

Louis Vuitton

Yves Saint Laurent

And for formal occasions, a *mignonne* scarf from *Hermès. C'est tout!*

Above all, I implore you to do everything
in your power to resist this fatal trio of
fashion *non-nons*:

Les bottines stupides (the stupid little booties)
Le pull bête d'hiver (the dopey winter sweater)
Le chapeau de cotillon ridicule (the silly party hat)

Need I add that the very suggestion of being seen in public attached to a "cat leash" is beneath discussion?

L'Allure

Beauty depends more on attitude than on looks.
To be thin, you must think thin and act thin. Pay
attention to your posture and demeanor —*tout votre
comportement*. Hold your chin up, keep your tail *levée*,
and never merely walk—promenade . . .

Never waddle—slink . . .

Never slouch—repose . . .

Never droop—lounge . . .

Never sulk—smolder . . .

And never pout—exact revenge.

Seasonal Cuisine

I regard hunting as nothing more than the pleasant task of browsing through the *merveilleux* open-air market in my own *jardin*. At every time of the year, there are *beaucoup de* yummy organic *entrées* out there, just for the asking.

And not only are these natural delicacies nutritious, but the exertion involved in "shopping" for them is quite aerobic, as they are truly "fast" foods!

In spring, there are
moles and voles,
plump and juicy . . .

In summer, baby bird's fresh from the nest . . .

In autumn, a whole
new litter of bunnies . . .

And in winter, the basement is a *véritable pâtisserie* of furry little things trying to escape the cold.

After you have made a selection, be sure to show everyone your *achat* (purchase). You are certain to be complimented on your excellent taste!

Three Light Dishes

Moles Marinière

SERVES ONE

INGREDIENTS

1 mouse
Pinch of
catnip

1. Sit outside mole hole.
2. When mole appears, pounce on it.
3. Add pinch of catnip.

Chickadee Fricassée

SERVES ONE

INGREDIENTS

1 baby bird

1. Pick up small baby bird freshly fallen from nest.
2. Remove unwanted parts.
3. Dice, cube, or slice into strips according to taste.

Shrewfflé

SERVES ONE

INGREDIENTS

1 shrew

1. Capture one good-sized shrew.
2. Bat it back and forth with paws for several minutes.
3. When it stops moving, it is done to perfection.

Healthy Habits

To promote a sense of well-being, we need to employ some tried-and-true restorative methods—what I call the five "musts" . . .

Adequate sleep

Regular naps

Plenty of rest

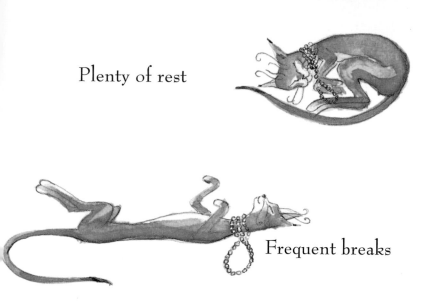

Frequent breaks

And ample quiet time

But do not fear—you will not become *une patate du divan* (couch potato) as long as you regularly intersperse your slumbers with a few calorie-burning "chairobic" activities.

Purring loudly . . .
50 calories

Giving yourself a bath . . .
175 calories

Digging your claws
into a cushion . . .
250 calories

Searching for a
missing cat toy . . .
400 calories

Covering the
entire surface of
the chair so that
no one else can sit
on it . . .
750 calories

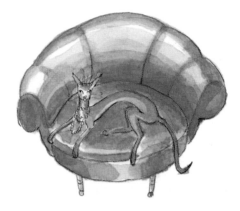

A Note of Caution

I strongly suggest that you avoid those fad diets dreamed up by *imbéciles diététiciens vétérinaires* where you subsist for an entire miserable month on something *complètement dégoûtant*, like moth wings, newt feet, and garden slugs.

Certainement, you will quickly shed a few pounds, but you will gain them right back once you succumb to the *irrésistible* temptations of the table.

Avant la diète

Durant la diète

Après la diète

I also urge you to pay no heed to the images produced by mirrors. They are calibrated for the bulkier human figure and simply cannot provide an accurate representation of a creature as *délicat* as a cat.

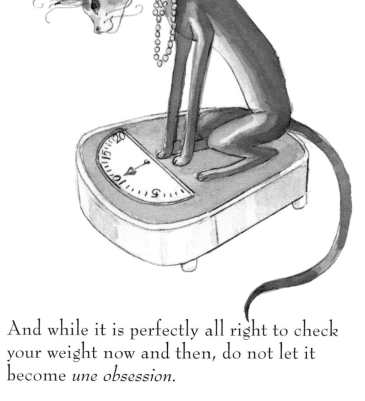

And while it is perfectly all right to check your weight now and then, do not let it become *une obsession.*

A better measure of your *physique* is what I call the "pillow test." Take a look at the impression you leave on a sofa cushion. It should be a faint, dainty imprint, not a bomb crater.

Oui

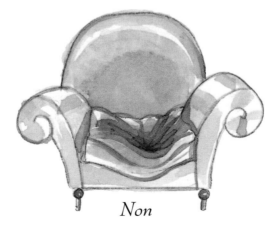

Non

Another highly reliable gauge of your *avoirdupois* is the *porte du chat*. As you exit, you should feel like a nymph emerging from a grotto . . .

Oui

. . . not a *saucisson* coming out of a sausage-making machine.

Non

Nos Petites Indulgences

Life would be very dull indeed if we did not permit ourselves the occasional sinful fling. *Par exemple,* cat grass is indeed toothsome, but there really is nothing like a prized houseplant.

The water in one's bowl is quite *rafraîchissante*, but *vraiment* there is no substitute for toilet water, the *champagne* of beverages.

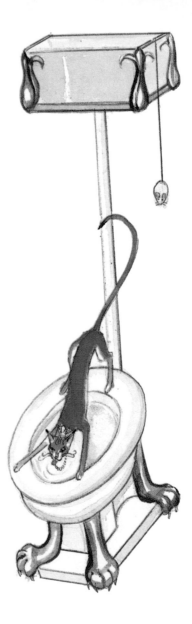

And even the ten-derest wild fledgling cannot compare with the sheer guilty thrill of a meal of pet *perroquet*.

Followed, perhaps, by a serving of succulent goldfish sushi. Incidentally, the energy expended in running away for a day or two after this *fête champêtre du chat méchant* (bad-cat blowout) transforms this lavish banquet of forbidden fruits into *cuisine minceur*.

La Joie de Vivre

I hope I have not left you with the impression that the French lifestyle is hard work. *Mes chéris*, nothing could befurther from the truth! It is just a question of employing commonsense strategies to get the most out of your daily rituals. For instance, wherever you go, always take the long way around.

Be *curieux* . . .

Vary your routine. As we say, *ne soyez pas un baton dans la boue* (don't be a stick-in-the-mud).

Be adventurous (though never fool-hardy). Explore your surroundings.

And while it is true that we may no longer have the peppiness or, *heureusement*, the appetite we had when we were kittens, we can still maintain a certain spark, an *élan*, a *je ne sais quoi* during each of our nine lives.

Un

Deux

Trois

Quatre

Cinq

Six

Sept

Huit

Neuf

Adieu

La Chatte Française, C'est Moi

- French cats don't do tricks.

- French cats don't come the first time
  they are called . . .
    or the second . . .
      or the third.

- French cats are not particularly eager
  to make the acquaintance of other cats.

- French cats despise arrogant, noisy,
  stupid French dogs.

- French cats don't beg (though they may
  make pointed requests).

- French cats prefer to remain in
  their *terroir*.

- French cats loathe being
  hauled around in cat luggage.

- French cats abhor the idea of being
  "fixed."

- French cats have a very broad definition of what constitutes a toy.

- French cats are affectionate, up to a point.

- French cats adore elegant shopping bags from expensive boutiques.

- French cats never break bric-a-brac, only expensive *bibelots*.

- French cats do not like to ride in automobiles.

- French cats need to disappear without a trace now and then.

- French cats always have a special hiding place.

- French cats can be mischievous, but never incorrigible.

- French cats insist that the litter box be cleaned regularly—if it is not, they will leave *petites cartes de visite* (kitty calling-cards) on the bathroom floor.

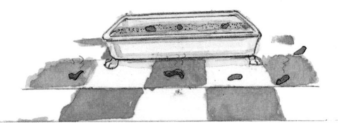

- French cats adhere to a strict, though largely indecipherable, schedule.

- French cats don't understand the meaning of the word *non!*

- French cats stray, but they usually return at mealtime.

- French cats don't sweat.

- French cats don't get wet.

- French cats fit in your lap.

- French cats don't get fat.